Log of Thrift Purchases

Date of
Purchase

What did
you buy?

Where did
you buy it?

Why did
you buy it?

Rate this
purchase 1-5

COST

ESTIMATED
SAVINGS

Log of Thrift Purchases

Date of Purchase

What did you buy?

Where did you buy it?

Why did you buy it?

Rate this purchase 1-5

COST

ESTIMATED SAVINGS

Log of Thrift Purchases

Date of Purchase

What did you buy?

Where did you buy it?

Why did you buy it?

Rate this purchase 1-5

COST

ESTIMATED SAVINGS

Log of Thrift Purchases

Date of Purchase

What did you buy?

Where did you buy it?

Why did you buy it?

Rate this purchase 1-5

COST

ESTIMATED SAVINGS

Log of Thrift Purchases

Date of Purchase

What did you buy?

Where did you buy it?

Why did you buy it?

Rate this purchase 1-5

COST

ESTIMATED SAVINGS

Log of Thrift Purchases

Date of Purchase

What did you buy?

Where did you buy it?

Why did you buy it?

Rate this purchase 1-5

COST

ESTIMATED SAVINGS

Log of Thrift Purchases

Date of Purchase

What did you buy?

Where did you buy it?

Why did you buy it?

Rate this purchase 1-5

COST

ESTIMATED SAVINGS

Log of Thrift Purchases

Date of Purchase

What did you buy?

Where did you buy it?

Why did you buy it?

Rate this purchase 1-5

COST

ESTIMATED SAVINGS

Log of Thrift Purchases

Date of Purchase

What did you buy?	Where did you buy it?

Why did you buy it?	Rate this purchase 1-5

COST

ESTIMATED SAVINGS

Log of Thrift Purchases

Date of Purchase

What did you buy?

Where did you buy it?

Why did you buy it?

Rate this purchase 1-5

COST

ESTIMATED SAVINGS

Log of Thrift Purchases

Date of Purchase

What did you buy?

Where did you buy it?

Why did you buy it?

Rate this purchase 1-5

COST

ESTIMATED SAVINGS

Log of Thrift Purchases

Date of Purchase

What did you buy?

Where did you buy it?

Why did you buy it?

Rate this purchase 1-5

COST

ESTIMATED SAVINGS

Log of Thrift Purchases

Date of
Purchase

What did
you buy?

Where did
you buy it?

Why did
you buy it?

Rate this
purchase 1-5

COST

ESTIMATED
SAVINGS

Log of Thrift Purchases

Date of
Purchase

What did you buy?

Where did you buy it?

Why did you buy it?

Rate this purchase 1-5

COST

ESTIMATED SAVINGS

Log of Thrift Purchases

Date of Purchase

What did you buy?

Where did you buy it?

Why did you buy it?

Rate this purchase 1-5

COST

ESTIMATED SAVINGS

Log of Thrift Purchases

Date of Purchase

What did you buy?

Where did you buy it?

Why did you buy it?

Rate this purchase 1-5

COST

ESTIMATED SAVINGS

Log of Thrift Purchases

Date of Purchase

What did you buy?

Where did you buy it?

Why did you buy it?

Rate this purchase 1-5

COST

ESTIMATED SAVINGS

Log of Thrift Purchases

Date of Purchase

What did you buy?

Where did you buy it?

Why did you buy it?

Rate this purchase 1-5

COST

ESTIMATED SAVINGS

Log of Thrift Purchases

Date of Purchase

What did you buy?

Where did you buy it?

Why did you buy it?

Rate this purchase 1-5

COST

ESTIMATED SAVINGS

Log of Thrift Purchases

Date of Purchase

What did you buy?

Where did you buy it?

Why did you buy it?

Rate this purchase 1-5

COST

ESTIMATED SAVINGS

Log of Thrift Purchases

Date of Purchase

What did you buy?

Where did you buy it?

Why did you buy it?

Rate this purchase 1-5

COST

ESTIMATED SAVINGS

Log of Thrift Purchases

Date of Purchase

What did you buy?

Where did you buy it?

Why did you buy it?

Rate this purchase 1-5

COST

ESTIMATED SAVINGS

Log of Thrift Purchases

Date of Purchase

What did you buy?

Where did you buy it?

Why did you buy it?

Rate this purchase 1-5

COST

ESTIMATED SAVINGS

Log of Thrift Purchases

Date of Purchase

What did you buy?

Where did you buy it?

Why did you buy it?

Rate this purchase 1-5

COST

ESTIMATED SAVINGS

Log of Thrift Purchases

Date of Purchase

What did you buy?

Where did you buy it?

Why did you buy it?

Rate this purchase 1-5

COST

ESTIMATED SAVINGS

Log of Thrift Purchases

Date of
Purchase

What did you buy?

Where did you buy it?

Why did you buy it?

Rate this purchase 1-5

COST

ESTIMATED SAVINGS

Log of Thrift Purchases

Date of Purchase

What did you buy?

Where did you buy it?

Why did you buy it?

Rate this purchase 1-5

COST

ESTIMATED SAVINGS

Log of Thrift Purchases

Date of Purchase

What did you buy?

Where did you buy it?

Why did you buy it?

Rate this purchase 1-5

COST

ESTIMATED SAVINGS

Log of Thrift Purchases

Date of
Purchase

What did
you buy?

Where did
you buy it?

Why did
you buy it?

Rate this
purchase 1-5

COST

ESTIMATED
SAVINGS

Log of Thrift Purchases

Date of Purchase

What did you buy?

Where did you buy it?

Why did you buy it?

Rate this purchase 1-5

COST

ESTIMATED SAVINGS

Log of Thrift Purchases

Date of
Purchase

What did
you buy?

Where did
you buy it?

Why did
you buy it?

Rate this
purchase 1-5

COST

ESTIMATED
SAVINGS

Log of Thrift Purchases

Date of Purchase

What did you buy?

Where did you buy it?

Why did you buy it?

Rate this purchase 1-5

COST

ESTIMATED SAVINGS

Log of Thrift Purchases

Date of
Purchase

**What did
you buy?**

**Where did
you buy it?**

**Why did
you buy it?**

**Rate this
purchase 1-5**

COST

ESTIMATED
SAVINGS

Log of Thrift Purchases

Date of Purchase

What did you buy?

Where did you buy it?

Why did you buy it?

Rate this purchase 1-5

COST

ESTIMATED SAVINGS

Log of Thrift Purchases

Date of Purchase

What did you buy?

Where did you buy it?

Why did you buy it?

Rate this purchase 1-5

COST

ESTIMATED SAVINGS

Log of Thrift Purchases

Date of Purchase

What did you buy?

Where did you buy it?

Why did you buy it?

Rate this purchase 1-5

COST

ESTIMATED SAVINGS

Log of Thrift Purchases

Date of Purchase

What did you buy?

Where did you buy it?

Why did you buy it?

Rate this purchase 1-5

COST

ESTIMATED SAVINGS

Log of Thrift Purchases

Date of Purchase

What did you buy?

Where did you buy it?

Why did you buy it?

Rate this purchase 1-5

COST

ESTIMATED SAVINGS

Log of Thrift Purchases

Date of Purchase

What did you buy?

Where did you buy it?

Why did you buy it?

Rate this purchase 1-5

COST

ESTIMATED SAVINGS

Log of Thrift Purchases

Date of Purchase

What did you buy?

Where did you buy it?

Why did you buy it?

Rate this purchase 1-5

COST

ESTIMATED SAVINGS

Log of Thrift Purchases

Date of Purchase

What did you buy?

Where did you buy it?

Why did you buy it?

Rate this purchase 1-5

COST

ESTIMATED SAVINGS

Log of Thrift Purchases

Date of Purchase

What did you buy?

Where did you buy it?

Why did you buy it?

Rate this purchase 1-5

COST

ESTIMATED SAVINGS

Log of Thrift Purchases

Date of Purchase

What did you buy?

Where did you buy it?

Why did you buy it?

Rate this purchase 1-5

COST

ESTIMATED SAVINGS

Log of Thrift Purchases

Date of Purchase

What did you buy?

Where did you buy it?

Why did you buy it?

Rate this purchase 1-5

COST

ESTIMATED SAVINGS

Log of Thrift Purchases

Date of
Purchase

**What did
you buy?**

**Where did
you buy it?**

**Why did
you buy it?**

**Rate this
purchase 1-5**

COST

ESTIMATED
SAVINGS

Log of Thrift Purchases

Date of Purchase

What did you buy?

Where did you buy it?

Why did you buy it?

Rate this purchase 1-5

COST

ESTIMATED SAVINGS

Log of Thrift Purchases

Date of Purchase

What did you buy?

Where did you buy it?

Why did you buy it?

Rate this purchase 1-5

COST

ESTIMATED SAVINGS

Log of Thrift Purchases

Date of Purchase

What did you buy?

Where did you buy it?

Why did you buy it?

Rate this purchase 1-5

COST

ESTIMATED SAVINGS

Log of Thrift Purchases

Date of Purchase

What did you buy?

Where did you buy it?

Why did you buy it?

Rate this purchase 1-5

COST

ESTIMATED SAVINGS

Log of Thrift Purchases

Date of Purchase

What did you buy?

Where did you buy it?

Why did you buy it?

Rate this purchase 1-5

COST

ESTIMATED SAVINGS

Log of Thrift Purchases

Date of Purchase

What did you buy?	Where did you buy it?

Why did you buy it?	Rate this purchase 1-5

COST

ESTIMATED SAVINGS

Log of Thrift Purchases

Date of Purchase

What did you buy?

Where did you buy it?

Why did you buy it?

Rate this purchase 1-5

COST

ESTIMATED SAVINGS

Log of Thrift Purchases

Date of Purchase

What did you buy?

Where did you buy it?

Why did you buy it?

Rate this purchase 1-5

COST

ESTIMATED SAVINGS

Log of Thrift Purchases

Date of Purchase

What did you buy?

Where did you buy it?

Why did you buy it?

Rate this purchase 1-5

COST

ESTIMATED SAVINGS

Log of Thrift Purchases

Date of Purchase

What did you buy?

Where did you buy it?

Why did you buy it?

Rate this purchase 1-5

COST

ESTIMATED SAVINGS

Log of Thrift Purchases

Date of Purchase

What did you buy?

Where did you buy it?

Why did you buy it?

Rate this purchase 1-5

COST

ESTIMATED SAVINGS

Log of Thrift Purchases

Date of Purchase

What did you buy?

Where did you buy it?

Why did you buy it?

Rate this purchase 1-5

COST

ESTIMATED SAVINGS

Log of Thrift Purchases

Date of Purchase

What did you buy?

Where did you buy it?

Why did you buy it?

Rate this purchase 1-5

COST

ESTIMATED SAVINGS

Log of Thrift Purchases

Date of Purchase

What did you buy?

Where did you buy it?

Why did you buy it?

Rate this purchase 1-5

COST

ESTIMATED SAVINGS

Log of Thrift Purchases

Date of Purchase

What did you buy?

Where did you buy it?

Why did you buy it?

Rate this purchase 1-5

COST

ESTIMATED SAVINGS

Log of Thrift Purchases

Date of Purchase

What did you buy?

Where did you buy it?

Why did you buy it?

Rate this purchase 1-5

COST

ESTIMATED SAVINGS

Log of Thrift Purchases

Date of Purchase

What did you buy?

Where did you buy it?

Why did you buy it?

Rate this purchase 1-5

COST

ESTIMATED SAVINGS

Log of Thrift Purchases

Date of Purchase

What did you buy?

Where did you buy it?

Why did you buy it?

Rate this purchase 1-5

COST

ESTIMATED SAVINGS

Log of Thrift Purchases

Date of
Purchase

What did
you buy?

Where did
you buy it?

Why did
you buy it?

Rate this
purchase 1-5

COST

ESTIMATED
SAVINGS

Log of Thrift Purchases

Date of Purchase

What did you buy?	Where did you buy it?

Why did you buy it?	Rate this purchase 1-5

COST

ESTIMATED SAVINGS

Log of Thrift Purchases

Date of Purchase

What did you buy?

Where did you buy it?

Why did you buy it?

Rate this purchase 1-5

COST

ESTIMATED SAVINGS

Log of Thrift Purchases

Date of Purchase

What did you buy?

Where did you buy it?

Why did you buy it?

Rate this purchase 1-5

COST

ESTIMATED SAVINGS

Log of Thrift Purchases

Date of
Purchase

What did
you buy?

Where did
you buy it?

Why did
you buy it?

Rate this
purchase 1-5

COST

ESTIMATED
SAVINGS

Log of Thrift Purchases

Date of
Purchase

What did you buy?

Where did you buy it?

Why did you buy it?

Rate this purchase 1-5

COST

ESTIMATED SAVINGS

Log of Thrift Purchases

Date of Purchase

What did you buy?

Where did you buy it?

Why did you buy it?

Rate this purchase 1-5

COST

ESTIMATED SAVINGS

Log of Thrift Purchases

Date of Purchase

What did you buy?

Where did you buy it?

Why did you buy it?

Rate this purchase 1-5

COST

ESTIMATED SAVINGS

Log of Thrift Purchases

Date of Purchase

What did you buy?

Where did you buy it?

Why did you buy it?

Rate this purchase 1-5

COST

ESTIMATED SAVINGS

Log of Thrift Purchases

Date of Purchase

What did you buy?

Where did you buy it?

Why did you buy it?

Rate this purchase 1-5

COST

ESTIMATED SAVINGS

Log of Thrift Purchases

Date of
Purchase

What did you buy?

Where did you buy it?

Why did you buy it?

Rate this purchase 1-5

COST

ESTIMATED SAVINGS

Log of Thrift Purchases

Date of Purchase

What did you buy?

Where did you buy it?

Why did you buy it?

Rate this purchase 1-5

COST

ESTIMATED SAVINGS

Log of Thrift Purchases

Date of
Purchase

What did
you buy?

Where did
you buy it?

Why did
you buy it?

Rate this
purchase 1-5

COST

ESTIMATED
SAVINGS

Log of Thrift Purchases

Date of
Purchase

**What did
you buy?**

**Where did
you buy it?**

**Why did
you buy it?**

**Rate this
purchase 1-5**

COST

ESTIMATED
SAVINGS

Log of Thrift Purchases

Date of Purchase

What did you buy?

Where did you buy it?

Why did you buy it?

Rate this purchase 1-5

COST

ESTIMATED SAVINGS

Log of Thrift Purchases

Date of Purchase

What did you buy?	Where did you buy it?

Why did you buy it?	Rate this purchase 1-5

COST

ESTIMATED SAVINGS

Log of Thrift Purchases

Date of Purchase

What did you buy?

Where did you buy it?

Why did you buy it?

Rate this purchase 1-5

COST

ESTIMATED SAVINGS

Log of Thrift Purchases

Date of Purchase

What did you buy?

Where did you buy it?

Why did you buy it?

Rate this purchase 1-5

COST

ESTIMATED SAVINGS

Log of Thrift Purchases

Date of
Purchase

What did
you buy?

Where did
you buy it?

Why did
you buy it?

Rate this
purchase 1-5

COST

ESTIMATED
SAVINGS

Log of Thrift Purchases

Date of Purchase

What did you buy?

Where did you buy it?

Why did you buy it?

Rate this purchase 1-5

COST

ESTIMATED SAVINGS

Log of Thrift Purchases

Date of Purchase

What did you buy?

Where did you buy it?

Why did you buy it?

Rate this purchase 1-5

COST

ESTIMATED SAVINGS

Log of Thrift Purchases

Date of Purchase

What did you buy?

Where did you buy it?

Why did you buy it?

Rate this purchase 1-5

COST

ESTIMATED SAVINGS

Log of Thrift Purchases

Date of Purchase

What did you buy?

Where did you buy it?

Why did you buy it?

Rate this purchase 1-5

COST

ESTIMATED SAVINGS

Log of Thrift Purchases

Date of
Purchase

What did you buy?

Where did you buy it?

Why did you buy it?

Rate this purchase 1-5

COST

ESTIMATED SAVINGS

Log of Thrift Purchases

Date of Purchase

What did you buy?

Where did you buy it?

Why did you buy it?

Rate this purchase 1-5

COST

ESTIMATED SAVINGS

Log of Thrift Purchases

Date of Purchase

What did you buy?

Where did you buy it?

Why did you buy it?

Rate this purchase 1-5

COST

ESTIMATED SAVINGS

Log of Thrift Purchases

Date of
Purchase

**What did
you buy?**

**Where did
you buy it?**

**Why did
you buy it?**

**Rate this
purchase 1-5**

COST

ESTIMATED
SAVINGS

Log of Thrift Purchases

Date of Purchase

What did you buy?

Where did you buy it?

Why did you buy it?

Rate this purchase 1-5

COST

ESTIMATED SAVINGS

Log of Thrift Purchases

Date of Purchase

What did you buy?

Where did you buy it?

Why did you buy it?

Rate this purchase 1-5

COST

ESTIMATED SAVINGS

Log of Thrift Purchases

Date of Purchase

What did you buy?

Where did you buy it?

Why did you buy it?

Rate this purchase 1-5

COST

ESTIMATED SAVINGS

Log of Thrift Purchases

Date of Purchase

What did you buy?

Where did you buy it?

Why did you buy it?

Rate this purchase 1-5

COST

ESTIMATED SAVINGS

Log of Thrift Purchases

Date of Purchase

What did you buy?

Where did you buy it?

Why did you buy it?

Rate this purchase 1-5

COST

ESTIMATED SAVINGS

Log of Thrift Purchases

Date of Purchase

What did you buy?

Where did you buy it?

Why did you buy it?

Rate this purchase 1-5

COST

ESTIMATED SAVINGS

Log of Thrift Purchases

Date of Purchase

What did you buy?

Where did you buy it?

Why did you buy it?

Rate this purchase 1-5

COST

ESTIMATED SAVINGS

Log of Thrift Purchases

Date of
Purchase

What did
you buy?

Where did
you buy it?

Why did
you buy it?

Rate this
purchase 1-5

COST

ESTIMATED
SAVINGS

Log of Thrift Purchases

Date of Purchase

What did you buy?

Where did you buy it?

Why did you buy it?

Rate this purchase 1-5

COST

ESTIMATED SAVINGS

Log of Thrift Purchases

Date of
Purchase

What did
you buy?

Where did
you buy it?

Why did
you buy it?

Rate this
purchase 1-5

COST

ESTIMATED
SAVINGS

Made in United States
Cleveland, OH
09 December 2025

28023539R00059